DANCES OF AUSTRIA

Plate 1   Schuastapolka, Salzkammergut

DANCES of AUSTRIA

KATHARINA BREUER

NOVERRE PRESS

ILLUSTRATED BY
ANNA WOLSEY
MUSIC ARRANGED FOR THE PIANO BY
FERDINAND RAUTER

First published in 1948

This edition published in 2021 by
The Noverre Press
Southwold House
Isington Road
Binsted
Hampshire
GU34 4PH

© 2021 The Noverre Press

ISBN 978-1-914311-16-1

CONTENTS

Illustrations in Colour, pages 2, 19, 30, 31
Map of Austria, page 6

AUSTRIA
BOHEMIA
MORAVIA
BAVARIA
UPPER
LOWER
TAUFKIRCHEN
LINZ
RIVER DANUBE
VIENNA
AUSTRIA
SALZBURG
ST. GILGEN
HALLEIN
EBENSEE
AUSSEE
STYRIA
SALZBURG
CARINTHIA
VORARLBERG
IMST
TYROL
BURGENLAND
ITALY
YUGOSLAVIA
Miles
0 10 20 30 40

The small and mountainous part of Austria which remained after the First World War as the Austrian Republic has a very old tradition of folk dance and custom.

During the time of prosperity in the long reign of the Emperor Francis Joseph, 1848–1917, this began to fade away. Peasant costumes were exchanged for town clothes, the young men found trousers more comfortable than their stiff and heavy leather shorts. The women, now able to reach the nearest towns easily by the newly built railways, saw town fashions, especially ladies' hats, which made a great impression on them. They of course began to wear them instead of their kerchiefs and bonnets. I remember as a child seeing peasant women making hay with fashionable straw hats perched on their heads.

But in the beginning of the twentieth century a few men who loved and understood the value of old traditions began to encourage the people to take these up again, and were helped in their endeavour by the wave of nationalism which broke over the land.

Austria, deprived of her large Empire, became aware again of her ancient peasant traditions, and clung to them more than ever. Leather shorts were worn again, gold-embroidered kerchiefs and bonnets, silken aprons and shawls were taken out of mother's bridal chest, and the old dances and customs were revived. In the first place it was perhaps to attract tourists, but a very strong second motive was to prove that the small Austrian torso still had a life of its own in spite of mighty neighbours on every side.

Peasant costumes, worn again by the rural population, even led the fashion, fanned by the thousands of visitors to the Salzburg Musical Festival, to the world-wide mode of the so-called Dirndl dress.

Austria has a great variety of ritual and recreational dances. The ritual dances, processions and many customs have survived from the Middle Ages and from far-off pagan times. The recreational dances have not such an ancient history and, in their present form, date from the beginning of the nineteenth century.

THE POPULAR LÄNDLER

Most of the present-day dance music is in Waltz or Polka rhythm, dating from the early nineteenth century, but one of the most widely known of Austria's Alpine dances, the Ländler, is thought to originate from a medieval Round dance. This, in its journey through the centuries, became a Pair dance in which the man leads the girl with complicated turns and twists to the final reunion of the pair in slow Waltz step. It is similar in most districts, but small differences inform the villagers immediately where the dancers come from. In Tyrol and Salzburg, for instance, this dance is called Schuhplattler, but still belongs to the Ländler family; in this form it is interrupted by the famous *Platteln*, rhythmical clapping of hands on knees, thighs, shoes and leather shorts, accompanied by stamping of feet. In some parts of Tyrol they add to this the *Trestern*, when the men leap high into the air or swing the girls above their heads.

In Styria the local form is the Steyrischer, in which the Waltz movement is interrupted by the men assembling in the middle of the dance hall, singing four-line verses, *Gstanzln* (from *stanza*), often with improvised words. These consist generally of mocking remarks about the girls or their men rivals, or complaints about the military life of conscripts. There is an enormous variety of these songs. In a village in Styria of barely a hundred inhabitants, Konrad Mautner, in his *Steyrisches Rasplwerk*, noted over 700 of these dance-songs. After every verse rhythmical clapping of the hands follows during 8 bars, and this clapping is very complicated. It works in the rhythm of threshing, and is absolutely polyphonic if one may so describe pure rhythm, with Vorpaschen, first voice, Zuahipaschen, second voice, Trittern, third voice, and Sextern, syncopating.

In Upper Austria this dance rhythm changed in the beginning of the nineteenth century from 3/4 to 4/4. In consequence the step is no longer a Waltz step, but a dignified walking step. In this new form the dance was taken up by the neighbouring Salzkammergut, where it is danced under the name of Ländler with special skill and perfection. This large family of dances derives its name from the part of Upper Austria known as *das Landl*, the little country. In fact the 4/4 version is called Ländler, whereas the 3/4 version under the name of Ländler became the ancestor of the world-famous Vienna Waltz. At the end of the eighteenth century, Danube barges going from Linz in Upper Austria to Vienna carried musicians on board; these were the Linz Quartettes. They played their regional dance-tunes in inns and at fairs, while waiting for their barges to return. The Viennese picked up the tunes, left out the complicated twists and grasps of arms, and copied only the end movement of the dance—the Waltz— holding the girls round the waist. It is hardly believable what storms of indignation were raised by this new and supposedly indecent dance. However, shortly afterwards, great composers such as Mozart, who was himself a very good dancer, began to write music for this new importation.

He called it the Deutscher (German dance), to underline
its difference from the old formal French dances such as
Minuets and Gavottes.

At the time of the Congress of Vienna, 1815, of which the
saying goes '*Le Congrès ne marche pas, il danse*', the Waltz was
already the height of fashion. Beethoven wrote many
Deutsche Tänze for the balls of the Congress members, and
Schubert brought this form to great perfection; it still went
under the name of Ländler, yet already was occasionally
called Waltz.

FROM FOLK DANCE TO BALLROOM

The history of the Waltz is a typical example of the way in
which folk dances turn into ballroom dances. In many
cases they find their way back to their original country
places and are reconverted into folk dances. To this
category belongs the Schottisch, one of the favourites in
Styria, Upper Austria and Salzburg. The peasants enjoy
this dance very much, especially when the musicians play
faster and faster, while at the end there is often such a
stamping, such a shrieking of girls swept off their feet, such
a yodelling by the menfolk, that one can hardly hear the
music. The Mazur is a free copy of the Polish Mazurka,
hands crossed as in figure-skating, partners whirling round
each other to change sides.

There are also ballroom forms reminding one of the
Polonaise, for instance the Schweinerne (Pig's dance) of
Salzburg, an opening promenade. The pairs walk in 4/4 in
a long procession through the room, clapping their hands
rhythmically. In Styria the host sometimes arranges a
Schneckentanz (Snails' dance). The company hold hands
in a chain, and to a lively march tune they are led through
the whole house, up stairs, through bedrooms, into attics,
until they finally end up in the dance-hall, where they
encircle the leader with shouts and laughter.

The end of many balls is the Polsterltanz (Pillow dance), adapted from eighteenth-century town dances, apparently a variant of the English Cushion Dance. The dancers form a circle while one man remains in the middle with a pillow in his hand, which he is to lay at the feet of his girl. But he first makes jocular attempts to persuade other girls to kneel on his cushion, pulling it away at the last moment for them to fall with their knees on the floor. At last he really drops the pillow, the girl kneels on it, the man does the same. He kisses her heartily and waltzes her round the room. The girl then takes over the pillow and performs the same ceremony, choosing one of the male dancers. This continues until nearly all the dancers have left the circle, whereupon the son of the house appears with a broom in his hand and, amidst great mirth, sweeps the last of the dancers out of the house. It is time to go home.

ALPINE DANCES

There are still old, simple peasant dances in 2/4 or 4/4 in the Austrian Alps. Some of their names indicate that they are descendants of seventeenth-century dances, for instance the Neukatholische (New Catholic) dance of Salzburg, supposed to have come into being after the Reformation when many returned to the Roman Catholic fold. It consists of holds, crossed arms at back or front of the dancers, steps, short jumps or stamping of the heels forwards and backwards, and finally Waltz or Polka step with arms round the partner's waist or shoulders. To this group belong the Hüetamadl (The Herd Girl), Neubayrische (New Bavarian), Siebenschritt (Seven Step) and others. Some are accompanied by dance-songs, old and new, showing that the peasant poet is still alive.

In the lower parts of the country, where harvest is more important than herding, there are no dances '*solang das liebe Getreide im Felde steht*', so long as the beloved grain stands in the fields. An exception is August 15th, the Feast of the Assumption, when the Almerinnen, the dairymaids with the herds on the high summer pastures, receive visitors from the valley below. Woodcutters and sportsmen and poachers, working and enjoying themselves in the mountains, will choose that day for a visit to the herds, and in the huts, or out on the glorious mountainside, informal dances are held to the sound of zither and ocarina. And when the sun has set, the snow-covered peaks take on the almost incredible rose-colour of the Alpine glow, and the guests depart with lovely two- and three-part yodels, or the Juchitzer and Alm-schrei, ancient cow calls, long-drawn-out yodels in a simple musical phrase, in very special melodic forms. The greatest day for the Almerinnen is in September, round about Mich-aelmas, when the herds are driven down from the high summer pastures to their dark stalls in the valley. The villagers go up to meet the flower-bedecked cattle on some clearing half-way up the mountain, the children are given special pastries made by the dairymaids for this occasion, and down in the valley that evening there is dancing at the inn to celebrate the home-coming—the Almtanz. The girls down from the Alp wear their white aprons, the village girls black or coloured silk ones, and Ländler and Schuhplattler are soon in full swing.

HARVEST AND VINTAGE

In the lower lands there are similar festivities for the harvest and vintage. I well remember how the grape-gatherers went from house to house in the outskirts of Vienna, where the famous Grinzinger and Nussberger vines grow, carrying the Vintage Crown covered with ribbons and flowers. They presented a glass of their new wine to the lady of the house, and danced a short Waltz with her outside the door.

High-lights in village life are shooting competitions and the Kirtag (Church Day), the feast of the Saint to whom the church is dedicated; but because of field work from dawn till dark throughout the summer days, these feasts are always postponed till September no matter what day is really that of the Saint. Then, when harvest is done and autumn ploughing not yet begun, the Church Day is held with old customs, games and dances. Amongst these customs is the Kufenstechen, a cavalcade on horseback, in the Gailtal. After this short relief from work no more dancing takes place, the days get shorter and the year draws to its end; only the Star Singers, one of whom bears a great star lighted through the darkness, appear just before Christmas with their traditional Nativity songs.

MEN'S DANCES

The men's dances still in practice in Austria can be divided into two categories: dances for amusement, and traditional dances with display of special skill, learned from closely guarded men's societies and performed on special days.

The amusement dances are very frequent in the mountainous forest districts. When a hard day's work is done, felling and hauling of trees, rounding-up of the oxen on the high slopes (the cows are always tended by dairymaids on lower grassy hills), the men assemble in their huts and cook their dinner very appetisingly—generally dumplings made in specially shaped spoons, accompanied by bacon and milk-soup. Then in the twilight they amuse themselves with games to test their strength, or with singing and dancing.

There is always a zither, mouth-organ, or guitar at hand. One of these men's dances is the Styrian Wischtanz executed by one or several pairs. The men hold an alpenstock between them, and to the tune of a slow Waltz they lift their legs rhythmically over the stick, twirl it above their heads and behind their backs, never letting go of it. As they keep their hats decorated with the chamois 'feather' on their heads while dancing, this needs great skill.

Another men's dance is the Buckeltanz, which is a mock Minuet, and must date from the time that formal ballroom dance arrived on the Alpine height. The tune is solemn and formal, and the dance consists of deep bows, either face to face or back to back. Of course there is joking and pushing going on, and it ends in a quick Polka round the dance space. The Tetscher is a Schuhplattler danced by men only in Salzburg and across the German frontier in Bavaria, where the *Platteln*, the clapping — and exceedingly hard clapping—is executed on the partner's posterior, while he is on all fours on the floor.

RITUAL DANCES

With the Sword dances we reach the ritual dances, those in the second category, appearing only on certain occasions and disappearing for the rest of the year. Austria is particularly rich in these, indeed she possesses some of the most remarkable in Europe. They nearly all appear during Carnival and during Carnival only, and behind the show and the skill there lies some deep-seated urge, which has brought them out for centuries past and which brings them out still.

I will begin with the salt-miners' Sword dance of Hallein, near Salzburg. This famous example has a 300-year-old history, and who knows how long an unwritten tradition before that? It is performed during Carnival by sixteen or twenty men and a leader wearing their mining costumes, white trousers and jackets, red sashes round their waists and black caps with white edges. The dance takes place in an open space lit up by torchlight; the music used to be drums and pipes but is now played by a brass band. The figures fall into line with the usual Europe-wide Sword dance, the men linked hilt-and-point and never letting go. But special figures depicting work in the salt mine are given, and at the end their flag, the leader bearing it hoisted high on the

14

swords, is 'swung', that is rhythmically waved in every conceivable manner and pattern.

A very similar example is from Hallstatt, another salt-mining centre, in Upper Austria, and more countrified but not less interesting Sword dances exist in the village of Laufenbach (where the Fool is hanged on the Lock of Swords), at Taufkirchen, at Ebensee and countless other places, to which must be added the Garland dances probably of the same stock and showing the self-same figures. Some of these got into the hands of the guilds and became very ornate, some continue in rustic style in the villages, and it is these which retain those strange folk figures, the Fools whose ribbons are torn off them by housewives, for they make the hens lay, the Animal-maskers, Bears, Goats, and so forth, which all come down to us from pre-Christian spring rites.

Perhaps the most remarkable of the seasonal dances are the extraordinary Schemen processions and dance-dramas also appearing during Carnival. *Schemen* is an old German word for ghosts or spirits; so it appears that these Carnival 'runners' represent the returned spirits who, for good or ill, come back to earth for one day at the turn of the year, pursued by friendly spirits who seek to protect the village and field from evil influences. Some companies are called *Perchten*, the followers of an ancient divinity Perachta, now sunk into a mythical old woman Frau Berta who is, however, still uncomfortably powerful on stormy nights. Perchten, like Schemen, can be both beneficent and malevolent, and curious it is, with memories of what was let loose on the world from the high fortress of Nazi rule, to perceive that Berchtesgaden in medieval German means the abode of the Perchten —certainly of the Evil Ones. They wear—their human representatives—all kinds of masks and carry great Alpine cow-bells to clang as they dance and run. Those at Salzburg wear towering headpieces six feet high and more, with flowers, looking-glasses and sham jewellery. Others wear

straw masks and tall pointed straw caps equally high, and
their movements are chiefly jumping, slow twirling and running. Often they are in two companies, the Schöne, beautiful, and the Schieche, ugly. The masks of these last are
positively terrifying. But the celebrated Perchten of Imst in
Tyrol are Roller, wearing small sleigh bells, and Scheller,
bearing enormous cow-bells, and with them go other companies, Spritzer, who squirt water over the onlookers,
Kubele Maien who do great execution with damp cloths,
and Hexen or witches who have their own dance. There is
some half-forgotten purpose in these wild doings, the squirting and wetting are efficacious rain magic, and the whole
thing is bound up with ancient notions of fertility rites in
early Spring, and the driving-out of Winter and Evil. Indeed the Imst people declare the years of the Schemen-
running are invariably years of good crops.

Again there are the Tresterer, wearing forty or more
white cock's feathers in their hats, whose rapid dance without more accompaniment than its own stamped-out rhythm
is a most impressive sight. Marks of their heels, high up on
the walls, are pointed out with awe and pride.

A WEDDING DANCE

Up to the sixteenth century the bride was handed over to
the bridegroom amidst traditional dancing which took place
even in the church. Bridal dances are still without number,
but only one can be selected, the Bandltanz (Ribbon dance),
the most colourful, widespread and attractive. The wedding Master of Ceremonies holds a pole from which hang
ribbons. The girls at the wedding hold each a ribbon and
plait them round the pole in various patterns, using the
usual Waltz step. This is not a Maypole, but one of those
innumerable *arbres d'honneur* as they are called in France,
carried about or stuck in the ground as a tribute to some
notable person—here the bride.

Most of the dances have instrumental accompaniment, beginning with the mouth-organ for improvised balls and finishing with the village band. The zither is a favourite instrument. As a rule Austrians are very musical and nearly everybody plays an instrument, so that village bands are easy to obtain. At the beginning of the nineteenth century the usual dance band consisted of two violins, a double-bass and a zither. Now flutes or clarinets are added, and the traditional zither will be replaced by an accordion. A tiny instrument, the Jews' harp, is never used for dances, but comes into its own when the young men go to woo their girls under their windows at night. This custom, which generally includes the right of entry through the opened window and goes by the name of *Fensterln*, reaches its culmination in the strange *Kiltgang* of the Swiss Alps. It has bred a whole cycle of 'Night Visit' songs, but the almost ghostly music of the little Jews' harp is said to be never-failing in its effect.

The words of dance-songs are frequently improvised by the singer and are satirical and cruelly critical in intent, probing into the scandals and gossip of village life, yet highly appreciated all the same—except perhaps by the person under review. These verses fit, or try to fit, the traditional tunes, and the dance continues all the time they are being sung.

Although there is immense variety in Austrian peasant costumes the basic forms are similar. They consist of long or short Loden—thick felt-like material—coats in grey, green or brown, in certain districts red, chamois leather shorts, knees bare or stockinged, woollen hand-knitted stockings in green, blue or white, heavily nailed boots or shoes, and a multiplicity of picturesque felt hats, adorned either with the

Gamsbart (chamois brush) or Scheibenbart (target brush), a chamois 'feather' arrangement round a centre of red cloth, embroidered with golden sequins, or feathers of black-cock, eagle or other birds. Waistcoats are of great splendour, in embroidered velvet, or gaily coloured cloth with long rows of silver buttons. Embroidered braces and richly ornamented leather belts are a great feature of the men's costumes, the embroidery often of feather quills.

Women's dress consists of a tight-fitting bodice of wool, cotton or velvet, laced or buttoned, over a white linen chemise with very rich short sleeves. Long sleeves, not embroidered but with a red braid at the wrists or elbows, go with certain costumes. A very full skirt in different colours and materials is worn with these bodices, with a silk apron for Sunday or a cotton one for weekdays. Head-dresses may be different in practically every valley. There are all sorts of felt hats, bonnets of gold or black lace, fur caps, black silk shawls or simple cotton handkerchiefs. Napoleon's invasion of Austria appears to have influenced headgear as well as leaving many a trace in village life. Women's Sunday clothes still show the once-fashionable Empire cut, high waist-line and long, narrow skirt. In Vorarlberg, the most westerly province, bordering on Switzerland, fur caps in the style of those worn by the Napoleonic guards still appear as women's—not men's—Sunday hats. Tradition says that some of these caps were thrown away by the retreating French army in 1809 and picked up by village girls who wore them in derision, to mock the would-be conquerors. They thus created a new fashion which has lived to be an old one.

Everywhere stockings are generally white, shoes black, in some districts with buckles.

Plate 2 Hüetamadl, Salzburg

FESTIVALS AND SEASONS WHEN DANCING MAY BE SEEN

Carnival	In Austria this season lasts from Twelfth Night to Ash Wednesday; so Maskers and Disguisers may be seen on Twelfth Night, and dancing on the Sunday, Monday and Tuesday before Lent. Imst, Salzburg and other Perchten dance-dramas lasting all day take place every three years (or should do so). Dates must be ascertained.
At Village Weddings	
Feasts of Village Patronal Saints (the Kirtag)	Always postponed till after harvest.
Feast of the Assumption, August 15th	On Alpine pastures at cheese-making huts.
About September 29th. Michael - mas Day	When the herds come down from the high pastures.
Harvest	
Vintage	
Shooting Competitions	

Steirischer Gebirgsverein	Graz, Styria
Naturfreunde-Jugend	„ „
Österreichische Jugendbewegung	„ „
Lehramtskandidaten	„ „
Österreichischer Turn- und Sport-Verein	„ „
Schüler der Bäuerlichen Fortbildungs-Schule in	
Gams ob Frauenthal	Styria
in Lichendorf bei Mureck	„
in St. Oswald ob Eibiswald	„
in Ligist	„

The Bundesstaatlicher Volksbildungs-Referent can give information about dance groups in Salzburg, Innsbruck, Linz, Klagenfurt and Vienna. The Staatsakademie für Musik in Vienna interests itself in folk music and dances.

THE DANCES

TECHNICAL EDITOR, MURIEL WEBSTER
ASSISTED BY KATHLEEN P. TUCK

ABBREVIATIONS
USED IN DESCRIPTION OF THE STEPS AND DANCES

r—right ⎱ referring to   R—right ⎱ describing turns or
l—left ⎰ hand, foot etc.   L—left ⎰ ground pattern
C—clockwise   C-C—counter-clockwise

For descriptions of foot positions and explanations of any ballet terms the following books are suggested for reference:

A Primer of Classical Ballet (Cecchetti method). Cyril Beaumont.

First Steps. Ruth French and Felix Demery.

The Ballet Lover's Pocket Book. Kay Ambrose.

REFERENCE BOOKS FOR DESCRIPTION OF FIGURES:

The Scottish Country Dance Society's Publications. Many volumes, from Thornhill, Cairnmuir Road, Edinburgh 12.

The English Folk Dance and Song Society's Publications. Cecil Sharp House, 2 Regent's Park Road, London N.W.1.

The Country Dance Book I–VI. Cecil J. Sharp. Novello & Co., London.

The dance holds described in the Steyrischer serve also for the Schuhplattler and the Ländler. In the latter dance, of which no description is given, there are many additional holds, the feature of the dance being the twisting and turning of the girl by the man into a great variety of positions.

The body is carried very straight and erect in all the slower dances, the men holding their heads high, the girls casting their eyes on the ground. In the livelier dances such as the Schottisch, Polka and Siebenschritt, the whole body, arms and feet are in lively movement. Good men dancers improvise jumps, wriggles and twists and shout loudly 'Juhu'.

BASIC STEPS

The Austrian basic steps are either Waltz or Polka according to the tune. The Waltz step is sometimes done with slightly inturned toes. A walking step is sometimes used in the Länder, while the Schuhplattler is characterised by the syncopated clapping of the thighs and slapping of the soles of the shoes.

DAS HÜETAMADL (*The Herd Girl*)

Region	Styria, Upper Austria and Lower Austria, where it is called Strohschneidertanz (the Strawcutters' Dance). This variant is from Salzburg. Plate 2.
Character	Lively.
Formation	Couple dance. Dancers stand side by side holding hands which are crossed behind their backs.

Dance	MUSIC *Bars*
1 Place outside foot forward on heel, bring it back to 1st position.	1
Place inside foot forward on heel, bring it back to 1st position.	2
Repeat this, doing it eight times in all.	3–8
2 Eight Polka steps turning, man's hands on girl's waist, her hands on his shoulders. At the beginning of the Polka the man may stamp his foot and both bounce on both feet to start.	9–16

Repeat the whole dance.

DAS HÜETAMADL

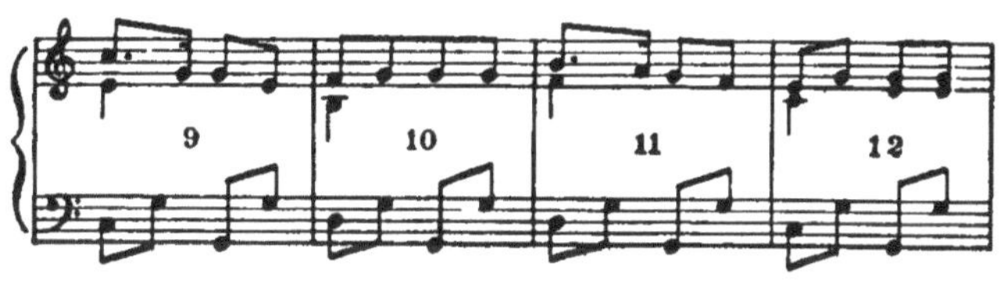

SCHUASTAPOLKA (*The Shoemaker's Polka*)

Region	Upper Styria. Salzkammergut. Plate 1.
Character	Mimetic.
Formation	Any number of couples and one odd man.

Dance	MUSIC *Bars*
Dancers find their partners and begin to polka round the room. When the odd man kneels down in the centre of the circle he mimes the action of the shoemaker, i.e. he holds his l hand on his chest as if holding shoe and with his r hand he pretends to pull the thread out to arm's length. As he does this he sings the dance song; all the men gather round him, join in the singing and clap their hands. The girls continue dancing round the room with either a Polka or a Walking step.	1–8 repeated

When the music stops the men spring up to find a partner and the odd man becomes the Shoemaker. The dance may be repeated as often as the band plays. The last man to be the Shoemaker is sometimes tossed into the air by the other men and has to buy drinks all round. As they toss him they sometimes sing the labour song—'Maker of Bridges' which is generally sung while driving piles into the river-bed.

The eight bars of music are repeated throughout the dance and mime.

SCHUASTAPOLKA

from UPPER STYRIA
Noted by Konrad Mautner

THE STEYRISCHER

Region	As danced in the district of Aussee, Styria. Plate 3.
Character	Dance, dance-song and syncopated clapping give variety and colour to this dance.
Formation	Couple dance followed by an informal grouping of the men in centre of circle while women continue to dance round the outside.

Dance	MUSIC *Bars*
INTRODUCTION	
The tune is played through while the men find partners and begin to waltz. When the cadenza is played the men let go of the women, who dance to the outside of the room to a circle formation followed by their partners. The men stand slightly ahead of their partners, inside hands joined and men's l hand in the small of their backs.	Steyri- scher 1–8 followed by Cadenza
THE HOLDS	
1 Each man pulls his partner in front of him with his r hand which he then raises to head height; he turns the girl once to her R under his arm; he turns the girl three times to her L under his arm.	1–8 repeated as often as desired
2 The man changes hands and leads the girl with his l hand so that she passes l shoulder with him, then behind his back placing her	

28

Generally played on the Zither

STEYRISCHER

CADENZA

Followed by Dance Song by men in three Parts
2nd time clapping without singing

DANCE SONG

29

Plate 3 and 4

(LEFT) *Steyrischer, Aussee*   (ABOVE) *Schuhplattler, Tyrol*

r hand in his r hand; he raises their joined
l hands over his head and turns the girl
to her L so that she faces him again with
both hands joined and crossed at head
height.

3 The man turns the girl half-way round to
her R; he then turns her half-way
round to her L; they drop hands, he
dances a whole turn to his R while she
turns to face him and they join in waltz
grasp—the girl's hands on man's shoulders,
his hands on her waist or behind her
shoulder-blades.

4 Couples waltz round room or on spot until
cadenza is played, when they pause.   Cadenza

5 The couples resume the waltz when the
tune begins again, but the men leave their
partners on the last bar and form a group   1–8
in the centre.
    The girls continue to waltz on the out-
side either alone or in pairs during the
Dance-Song.

THE DANCE-SONG   Dance-
1st time. One man begins to sing the dance-   Song
song which the other men take up—some   1–8
in falsetto treble, some taking the other
two parts.

2nd time. The music of the dance-song repeats
but the men join in with hand-clapping   1–8
instead of singing, the same first man still
leading. The clapping is done in varying

syncopated rhythms, the whole effect supposed to represent the rhythm of threshing.

Variation. The singing and clapping is repeated three times unless one of the men
shouts 'Hua-Whoa' when the clapping is
continued for 24 bars instead of the usual
8. In this case the clapping is done at first
in the syncopated rhythm, but later with
an even continuous clap.

The men spring up, take their partners and
start the dance from the beginning.

The Steyrischer therefore consists of
repetition of dancing, singing and clapping.
These are repeated five or six times to
make a complete Steyrischer. The dance
is always repeated with the same partner
with one exception : towards the end of the
evening the band may be asked to play a
Steyrischer Auf-Pasch. Then, after each
turn of dance, the song is sung once and
the clapping done for only 8 bars, after
which each man takes his neighbour's girl
and this continues until every man has
danced with every girl.

For each round of dancing a few pence
are paid to the band.

THE SCHUHPLATTLER

Regions	Tyrol, where it is famed at Kitzbühel and Kastelruth. At Salzburg, St. Gilgen and parts of Upper Austria; also across the German frontier in Bavaria and across the Italian frontier. Plate 4.
Character	The dance is described as the strutting of the cock in front of the demure hen.
Formation	Couple dance.

Dance

<table>
<tr><td></td><td></td><td>MUSIC
Bars</td></tr>
<tr><td>1</td><td>The girls waltz slowly round the room while the men waltz round them (each round his partner) with clucking and hissing sounds in imitation of the black cock.</td><td>A</td></tr>
<tr><td>2</td><td>Partners waltz round the room, men's hands on girls' waists and girls' hands on men's shoulders.</td><td>B</td></tr>
<tr><td>3</td><td>The girls waltz round alone while the men perform the Platteln in the middle of the circle.</td><td>A</td></tr>
</table>

PLATTELN OR SCHUHPLATTLER STEPS

1	3 short stamps	1 bar.
2	Slap soles of shoes and thighs alternately (1 & 2 & 3 &)	3 bars.
3	3 short stamps	1 bar.
4	Slap soles and thighs as before, finishing with a high leap	3 bars.
	Repeat all or improvise	8 bars.

SCHUHPLATTLER

KASTELRUTH, TYROL

35

Clever dancers improvise every kind of slap—head, cheeks, calves, etc. They also turn somersaults between the slaps, turn Catherine wheels and do other gymnastics exactly in time.

4 Partners waltz round the room as in Fig. 2.   B

5 Repeat Fig. 3, finishing the whole dance with the men leaping high into the air.   A

AN EXAMPLE OF A SCHUHPLATTLER RHYTHM

There is no one traditional rhythm but the following version shows the continuous half-beat rhythm which is characteristic.

Stand with feet in 2nd position, knees slightly bent:

	MUSIC
	Bar 1
Smack r thigh with r hand	Beats: 1
,, l ,, ,, l ,,	and
,, the inside of l foot, which is raised across the r leg, with r hand.	2
,, l thigh with l hand	and
,, r ,, ,, r ,,	3
,, l ,, ,, l ,,	and
	Bar 2
,, outside of r foot, which is raised sideways, knee slightly bent, until leg is nearly horizontal, with r hand.	Beats: 1

Smack l thigh with l hand.
" r " " r "   and
" l " " l "   2 and
" inside of l foot with r hand.   and 3
" l thigh with l hand.   and
Repeat above movements as often as desired.

The movements can be done on the spot as described, but are often worked up with a steady step-hop on alternate feet, raising the l leg across the body while hopping on the r, and raising the r leg sideways while hopping on the l. The step-hop is continuous throughout the three-beat rhythm and should first be practised to counts of 1 and 2 and 1 and 2 and. When danced to 3/4 time the actual hop comes on the following beats:

1 and 2 and 3 and 1 and 2 and 3 and
    Hop   Hop   Hop

We beg you not to think of regional costumes as fancy dress. They are held in honour by their wearers as an important part of their heritage. Respect them. Do not dress dancers in a make-believe Tyrolese costume for the Styrian dances. You would be equally justified in dressing a Helston Furry dancer in a Highland kilt.

The Editor

BIBLIOGRAPHY

ALFORD, VIOLET, and GALLOP, RODNEY.—*The Traditional Dance*, London, 1935.

EMMERICH, KARL.—*Berchtesgadner Almtänze.* Berchtesgaden, 1906.

MAUTNER, KONRAD.—*Steyrisches Rasplwerk: Vierzeiler, Lieder und Gasslreime aus Gössl am Grundlsee.* Vienna, 1910.
Alte Lieder und Weisen aus dem Steiermärkischen Salzkammergut. Vienna, 1910.

PETER, ILKA VON, and LAGER, HERBERT.—*Perchtentanz im Pinzgau.* Vienna, 1940.
Tänze aus Österreich. Vienna, 1946.

REITER, POMMER and ZACK.—*Alpenlieder aus Deutsch-Österreich.* (100 songs and 60 folk dances, from Carinthia, Styria and Tyrol.) Leipzig and Vienna.

WEILEN, E. VON (ed.).—*Die Österreichisch-Ungarische Monarchie in Wort und Bild.* 24 vols., 1886–1902.

WOLFRAM, RICHARD.—'Tanz im Volk', in illustrated monthly *Die Pause*. Vienna, 1939.
Schwerttanz und Männerbund. Kassel, 1936–38.
'Ritual and dramatic associations of Sword and Chain Dances.' *Journal of the English Folk Dance and Song Society*, vol. II, 1935.

ULRICH, HERMANN.—*Der Wiener Walzer.* Free Austrian Movement cultural series. London, 1940–46.

ZODER, RAIMUND.—*Das Deutsche Volkslied.* 10 vols. Vienna, up to 1943.

Film.—Unser Alpenvolk und seine Lieder. Urania. Vienna.